"Arranged in four movements revealing a classical symphonic form with its movement's tempos and use of thematic material, this is a reflective but attentive set of impressions: images of the existence and decay in the human-made world, with the strength and architecture of the underlying nature that these inhabit.

This is not commentary. The poem's structure is also its content, also a reflection of the words it contains.

A rhythm appears, it dissipates,
a rhyme appears, it dissipates.

The reader is left with the memory of the images conjured during the reading, of places and things, and of ghosts lurking within them.

I always admire poets, these people who can elicit these layers of meaning simply by means of some specific arrangement of words."

-Jonathan Segel (Musician and Composer)

"This is a great poetic picture of life on our planet. Constructed like a symphony in four movements, it has a real structure, like a great work of classical music. I was able to find the time over three days and nights to read the whole epic poem CAREFULLY and really admire such devotion to the English language while being able to chronicle these crazy times!!!"

Write on! …Write on! …

-David Amram (American Composer)

"As the title of this collection suggests, the words of Jim D. Deuchars have long contained a strong sense of musicality and playfulness. On the page, they are nothing short of visual theater and while past work often moved toward the more experimental, Symphony in B flat major offers a more linear narrative that will leave the reader breathless, and on the edge of their seat, like the twist and turns of a river, these are wild words for uncertain times."

–John Dorsey (Author of *Dead Photographs*)

Symphony in B flat major

Poems by Jim D. Deuchars

Luchador Press
Big Tuna, TX

Copyright © Jim Deuchars, 2025
First Edition: 1 3 5 7 9 10 8 6 4 2
ISBN: 978-1-958182-92-5
LCCN: 2025937982

Author photo: Jim D. Deuchars
Forward by Holly Day

Table of Contents:

Forward

In the early 19th century, musicologist Ernst Pauer published a series of texts that assigned emotions to musical keys. He wasn't the first to do so--Christian Schubart's 1806 publication "Ideas for an Aesthetics of Music" also assigned feelings and emotions to musical keys, and before that, Johann Mattheson wrote extensively about it in 1713. Of course, all three "borrowed" the concept from the ancient Greeks and then attached their name to the concept, as musical theorists are often wont to do. But Pauer was the first to truly popularize the concept, most likely through a series of textbooks and articles that he probably forced his students to read and later quote at fancy cocktail parties.

The preceding paragraph has nothing to do with this book, except that it explains the title of the work as a whole. According to Pauer, the quality expressed by the chord and scale of B flat major is "an expression of quiet contemplation." The four poems in this book—mirroring the four parts of a symphony--take the reader through a series of contemplations on industrial landscapes, the tumultuous passage of a river, and the malleable power of and eventual uselessness of words.

You don't have to like classical music or know anything about music theory or give a crap about 18th or 19th century music theorists to enjoy this book—this is all self-indulgent rambling on my part. Books are for reading, and for losing yourself in, and for driving you to that place of quiet contemplation B-flat major is supposed to be responsible for. And that's what this is for. All of it.

-Holly Day (*Music Theory for Dummies*)

For CBP

The fourth dhyana is a state of perfect purity and peace, in which the mind is above all gladness and grief. Be sober and abandon wrong practices which serve only to stultify your mind.

Andante espressivo

Sing a song of six packs
a gullet full of rye
awakened in the heartland
an exquisiteness of sky
falls slowly to horizon;
golden, amber, yellow,
beige and tans
that once were greens
recede to grey of city's smoke.
Morning's brontosauran reds
of smokestack blight
recede to grey of night
and concrete roadways
sigh their way to factories
sinister in the clang and crash of metal
'til the press of steel into
specific shapes and weights
betrays a sudden, gentler rolling
gradually decaying
into wind and shit
of time's effect
on generation after generation
degenerating slowly
to the compost undercarriage
of a misshaped family tree;
branches bent in light of sound
like swirling wind in sea-shelled ear.
The snowed out rush of ocean's
constant muttering's
the distant freeway's rumble;
engines drunk on gasoline
demean the speeding sight
obscene:

our need to be:
there.
now.

Feeling shell-shocked in the promised land and
crowded cloudly into children's prayerful circles,
these unshaved skeletons of combs
and sawed-off broom handles
seem wryly strung together
wily
billowing in bellowing wind
like an archaic necklace
dragged by anchor of
an antiquated image
seen as icon carved in ivory
rattling its bits in air
now being blown beneath the sidewalks
until rippling it
rips it up through cracks.

The skins of old autos
and the guts of the bicycles of youth,
flung far and anonymous
along the street's encouraged murals,
juxtaposing yellow spots
and whitish lines
while quivering arrowly and narrowing
into a Miles Davis slant
crossing greenish lines
and plastered onto frescoes
of factory walls
on street corners caustic

in the scatter of cement dust:
salt and pepper for the dispossessed.

The Interstate's not interesting to those
who summarize their days
in sundry gossip's local throes;
what business of teenagers
conjuring such earnest manifestoes?

How absolutely lustrous in their gloom,
all the while monstrous and maniacal;
these sketched-out letterings
and backways-leaning efforts
at some miscommunication
plague the nation.

This mode becomes a mania
manic in its pandemonium;
sonic is its doom
so know the monster!
Know the fiendish monster you have with
out sheer astonishment
of uptight oversights
and words that mean one thing
and then another:
be assured
we're high enough to grasp at breath
'cause breadth of meaning

(possible and otherwise)
grows oversized
and presses down against our lungs.

We're wordless
and we've now
surpassed the timberline;
there is no highpoint, apex,
scenic overlook nor precipice
from which to stagger down
(and unenlightened)
until this foolish husk,
the scarecrowed skin of man,
is stretched across indifferent bones.

The bones!

The bones!

The cats will choke on chicken bones
then rest 'neath hidden piles
of some preselected stones
(and mewling moans)
all the while beguiling
'til they're gone to dust and bones.

And how that dust will grow.

And how that dust will blow ye forward.

Go ye toward the unwrit absurd
and cast yer wordy spells
encrypt;
encoded in a downcast voice
broadcast wide
and modified like worms in rain

that has no cause
nor reason to encourage
lithesome motion.
Frightened lifeless clouds emerge
into a merge of shapes,
uncanny sizes grown to drapes
obscuring even contemplation's
mindless urges.

Go thee now and teach of lands unreached
(in fact, these sands grow better castles
depending on the teller of the tale).
After each retelling tooled and telephoned
into intent epochal obfuscations
almost optimistic in their glee;
can we be made much colder
by the regularity of nightcome's fall?

These cooler episodes bring shades of sleep.
Ensuing dreams may rush
to conjure brooding ancient
swastikas of sweats
or new and sweetly energetic actions
bent on burning
like a firefly at dusk among the lilacs.
That greenish blur is so like truckstop's glowing sign
we are reminded that the diesel smudge of dark
can only hint at heat that will astonish
in the pure unbroken sunlight
on the blacktops of tomorrow and her kin.

The wind shades more
a snarling brush or snare
and drier
in the leaves and pages
not as green as we once thought they seemed,

the rain's no cause for much
but encouraging the over-ripe
to linger.

Weather's ancestry is multivaried
(as a soundtrack of Olympic chaos ought to be).

Terraces of mountain's gardens fall to pull of gravity.
Coffee beans will roll downhill to other observations.
We will still (and random) chew on barks and leaves,
spit the seeds erratically
about our NOW nativity.
With gravest reservations
we await the BOOM
of unkind word's
reverberations;
remembering and repeating
every fleeting incarnation we assume.

So be it

corn or carrots
Brussels sprouts or beans,

perchance: alfalfa!

The wind and rain destroy
and toy with us
and with the toy within us.
The rain and wind grow mean
…and spirited;
that is
if they deign
to reign at all.

So be it.

Pretty words
that once were all out loud
are strangely quiet now;
secluded in bookended dens.

Having outgrown habit's lens
while accidently straying
into wordless worlds of gods
we let angelic verbs take lead.
At once despair,
then emptiness replaced itself
with faceless vagrancies of dire truth
and anger, tears unshed
embedded selves in sound.

When clouds fall to the ground
be kind,
for gods are sure to walk about
in fogs like these.

In fogs like these
the silence of the thickened air
becomes impossible to breathe.

When time's not such a luxury perceived
it becomes impossible to take
each separate moment,
lay it side the next and last
and stretch to an entire day.

Words take place

(as only colors should)

through shell
replacing heart
and gut
and ear
and now
we've only left our eyes

(and reading words
sends us to sleep!)

Now the compass
points us to the wheel we were
a-wondering why (aloudly).
Fortune's pill (our free will)
is swallowed up in earthly arms
as if a multitude of wandering nonsense birds
betrayed the sky to salve the sinking mood of man.

Listening to birdcall's
stutter into wordfall's
wicked stricture;
a system of communication's borne.
Birdsongs outmaneuver car horn's
smooth delay; beware:
the ass-end of our interaction's
farting bland repeated details
filling hours--

even squeezing every minute from the day!

even ringing in and out the next!

And while the band played on (and on
(e'er white noise felt at all sublime))
and once we'd heard the sizzling dawn
the crooner'd made the language rhyme.

After we had taken pains
and having prayed
and brayed
in smokestained buses
passing selfnamed
selfsame
smalltown
shopping strips

and as we drove
(more accurately: were driven)
we enriched victors
clarified our history

(in fact, every thing that's left is history):
the manners and the messages;
long passages concerning ways
we've shaped our tongue.
And on such cold paper.

How overwhelming!

When one's disposition
can be traced to a specific moment
and a solitary word,
certain smells remind us of less hopeful days
when life so liberally and literally
taken to extremes of heat and chill and emptiness
burst like stroke drowns brain
in pools of unproved thought
'til nag of raw emotion clots as time blanks eyes;
as ice of will
(one needling step each day)
fades the silhouette of memory
into blue of night
embalmed in words,
perceptions,
taken ever out of context.

The English Language is a very large one.

Each man understands his words
and misperceives another's.

How language is perverted!

Perversion's curse is verse
as commentary
and bullshit
of our worldly-worded romance.
Our romantifiction's just
unjust cause for pale romance's smooth cessation.

New romantic factions
factor in the actions
of the rootless
and the dear:

here we depart.

> Such romantic construct
> now and here
> refuted be.

The fine time of all our
(unkind!) fighting frightened minds
unwind our broadwinged sorrows,
unfolding into flotsam;
sometimes fetching, even finicky,
aflutter, feathery at times,
revolving 'round uncertain words
evolving into flight
of dusty, winded wordsong's might.

We thought we had need of a dictionary
to record these terms in contract;
to make more clear the 'why' and 'how',
the 'such' that construct shall contract

to fit our tightened vocal chords,
but rhetoric's regardless echo logic
was the key;
rationalizations
rationing out ecology
and fattening into lists and diaries:
a library is just a diarrhea.

Who'll remember crumpled,
balled up scatterings of lines of symbols
once these pages
mortal out
into forgotten,
fallen leaves?

And what of future songs that rave about us?
In a desperate craze of scribbling hands
this new, collective voice
will rage about on what we've done
to fill the silence,
recording for posterity
our wiggling ink lines;
forests sacrificed in violence.
Is their dead instruction loud enough
to offer any guidance?

Such romantic construct
now and here
refuted be.

Reeling off a run-on sentence of a road,
waggling in tensed nonsense,

we are completely hooked and blind
while reading silent letters.
Instead, see here:
while seeing all
and hearing
slightly
more (or more or less)
we're realized as colors fast,
phonetically alive
and wide
and ranged
along the prairie.
Linguistic breadth
has come about
and come to this,
and thus appears
the sum of 'us'
upon these rough-hewn pages.
Books result from genocide of trees;
the flattened forest
stumped
by rage of
previously mentioned
unkind wind--
this war to end all:
a war of Words.

Defenselessly,
in pieces...
our language grows.
Each makes his march-like step
and is made great
and left anonymous.

All who added words
lent new sounds
(and some unsound choices)
that led to voices'
ceaseless noises.

Sentence structure's stretched
to fit our modern scientific pretense;
past was just a prelude;
now we're smothered
in a motherlode of language;
oppressive fatherland
of all our wicked 'ologies'
ain't nothin' but a sad day's vacant lot,
a weary, brave Metropolis;
our overarching scar tissue tongue
is done;
wedged and staid
in brackish waters
leaning city-like against the great
and placid shoulder of edgy
misdirected waterways;
how we've misguided
all we've done;
everything
we stumble on
and spit up
into local skies.

Such vocal cries!

The hollow crack
of bone against bone!

The surprising drift to dust!

And so we rise
like clouds of thought balloons
lifted off the edge and slowly turning
'til we scatter in the lofty altitudes
of our misbegotten attitudes
for once we've gone this high,
no telling thence
what might come real.

Such romantic
indiscretions
undisputedly
refuted be.

Practiced words
beat rhythmic steps
along the walk.

On delivery
they seldom rhyme.

We had hoped
these heavy syllables
would break through
seething window's panes
enlightening the cobwebbed room.

They fell as quickly to the floor

like a pendant on a chain
whose clasp had given out

and given in to tug
of weighted seconds passing.

The terror of each moment's breath.

The beastly tock of minute's hand's
another day gone by.

It's the dread of sleepless nights
that stirs us from our sleep each night
and hope that seals the unsure,
obscured mornings
where a pimple of a sun
busts through the clouded skin of sky.

So here and now
such
romantic misconception
must
most desperately
misconcocted be.

Understand:
words are all
relatively scant of substance.

And that which illumines
or makes clear the mind
may sometimes come down suddenly
or forcibly;

may finally pass through torturous days,
descend and rest,

perch or settle into dust;
may be quick to come
and may arrive by chance;
may brilliant be or pale
or even fail to solve eventually
as color waiting constantly to happen.

Just as incense burns beneath an open window,
smoke will, on occasion,
for a bleak and empty instant
fall into a brave collision's vicious tide.
The potency of fear pools still at ankle's depth
beneath the rippling strobe's electric OHM!

And still,
as iced o'er pools do spare us, on our trek,
from fish's doom, the smoke's disjointed screaming
streams a lighter shade than outside's nearly
green-grey skies can conjure.

Such romantic construct once begun
be gone
until we sing our songs suspenseful,
empty pockets running dry. Asleep
or waking on a heartland highway indecisive,
surprised upon a road of word-like sounds
we try to understand
the vivid instincts of the sky
to change complexion.
Our disposition's predisposed to wander
through the noises that our throats can shape.

There are voices of action
and expressions of consequence
and persons
having only ever wanted
of a nearby heartbeat.

Is the Fourth Dhyana
really meant to be so sad?

When
in the course of human months
and humane ears
one's thinking
sets into a process
images,
imaginations
and
imaginary words
upon a blank,
uncaring,
unencumbered canvas…
one's inherent madness
(at its absolutest)
best is heard
in works of speech
in crowds.

Greyhound's
ache of rumble
wakes aweary
halfway sleepers (outside time)
from slumbers

full of biting naked
stunning
(vivid) dreams.

Sleep comes off and on by light switch
in the morning's Allegheny mist
where Brigadoon that hums as truckstop
blurried white decays
into the frequency of light (as thought).
Such winds chafe lips
and shiver ash from cigarettes.

We sing
a song of six packs
a gullet
full of rye,
awakened
in the heartland
an exquisiteness of sky
falls slowly
to horizon;
golden, amber, yellow, beige and tans
that once were greens recede
to grey of city's smoke.
Morning's
brontosauran reds
of smokestack blight
recede
to grey of night
and concrete roadways

sigh their way
to factories

sinister
in the
clang and crash
of metal
'til the press of steel
into
specific shapes and weights
betrays
a sudden, gentler rolling
gradually decaying
into wind
and shit
of time's effect
on generation
after generation
degenerating
slowly
to the compost
undercarriage
of a
misshaped
family tree.

We're stuck
(within the glow of dawning's
salmon ardor)
with almost a million words
(and that's just in the book we reference now).

Such a shape!

Such a size!

The sheer enormity
can stretch the skin of sound
until this dialogue's balloon
bursts diabolical and
not quite unexpectedly.
Expectant, though,
and introspective
as the slowly blinking flash
of our most colorful expressions
leaves us unsilent
and without a thing to say.

The chill sets with our sun these days
these days when winds regard the smoke
the smoke of breath in air, in err,
and e'er we act as if sheer will
felled trees.

Largo

Let me tell you a story about a river:

sprung loose
into dramatic
mountain birth,
a
trifling seep
that
drips
her way
through
cracked breach
of granite,
shale
or
sentimental
sediments.

The
anxious quality
of such
chill-awakened
water
precipitates
a
longing lurch
descent
to Mother's
oceanic womb.
This
cold spring

crib,
so sluggishly she seeps,

swells, heaves
tectonically,
pulled
out of
harmful reach--
a sleepy
sea bed
tossed,

then made into
a mountain top,

the
bloodless thirst
of seawall
willed
into
a dry
and
damning
doom
of precipice;

streaming veins
discussing comforts
of the sea
we all
crawled out;
we're sliding

(mildly

wildly,

gliding)

violently impatient
foaming
at the
water's fall
even oddly
unaware but
following
a sudden
and
persistent path
unevenly;

(believe

you,

me!)

she's
even
more severe
when
annually

over-laden
with the
leaden
chill
of massive
snowmelt avalanche's
mad advances
wiping
years away
like tears;

the
way
they

smoothly suffer
wondering
when chance
will sob
the day
away
into
a riverfall
of such
spectacular rebirth,

unsettling
pebbles
leave pools
defenseless

embittered

raging
brave and
gravely
into a
contrary tug

ever present

as she
pulls
at steelhead,
forced
in
violent turns
against earth's

barren
terms of
gravity
upstream
until
misfortune's
pinwheel spins
into a
dark idea

and
we
damn her
in
relentless rush
of

rash decisions

having given

little thought

we'd run

into such

choke

of

purple loosestrife

such a

teaming

puddled

gauntlet

of

gradual resistance

teasing us;

urging us

to swirl

and

goading us

to

purge ourselves

of

spiraling regret:

emerging

almost worried,

wary

as a

bittern,

tentative
as dusk:

as if
approaching night,
we
had begun
to understand the

wonder...

This is not such a river.

Rolling slow
and
brooding large

and
largely

unconcerned

in
wafting laze
of
twilit days;

amazing drift
of
afternoons arrayed

on rafts
delayed
by
soft spots
in the
cloudballs
until,

approaching
shoreside thicket,

our landing
is betrayed
by
Canada's
Cruel Geese.

Alarming honk
bleats
mad disturbance
in the
seamlessness
of passing
lifestill hours

until time
astonishes herself
loosed
and
meandering by
countless moments,

unmentionable misdeeds,

vivid,

whispering reeds;

a half light

glimmering
unrepentant
thick
of humid air
ensnaring
clouds of
marsh mosquitoes

snapped up
glidefully
by
swarm-discounting
swifts

until
we wish
that world
away

in whirling waves
twisting shadows

slithering
somewhere

between blue
and indigo

and

purple,

&
backlit
by a
dreamsicle sunset,

Great Blue Heron.

                          Still.

                                A
                              mad
                              silk rain
                              melts
                                into
                              a drop
                              of sky

           then floats
           into

           a haze

of misperception,

                              stalled
                            enthralled
                              and all
                                 in all
                            depressed
                        against
                        the dulled
                    sheen skin
                              of
                        whispering
                    surface tensions.

        The still
          that sets
      in mud
        on bank
          slurps oozing
      underneath,
          between
  bare toes.

                              In a
                        drier age
                        than this

              and
            countless
                centuries
          from now,
                        the memory

of
this path
long disappeared,

a
sudden stumbling
in earnest
upon this
ancient footprint
by some
lonely anthropologist
will spark
new speculations,
will birth
enlightened conversations,

will
torment
the angry
scientist

with
a flood
of
low recriminations
and acrid
false
apologies.
Meanwhile
the
stilted hissing
of
still breathing's

                                still
                              enough
                                   to startle
                                   grebe.

                    Great Blue Heron.

Undistracted.
                                        Even as
                                    becalm of kiss
                                    becomes
                                      most
                                  unbecoming
                                    almost
                                        clever
                                      as the
                                    wind cries
                                  songs of
                                wanderlust

                    and wonder

                              lost;

                        when yonder

                    knotted wanderless
                              in a
                        willow's tendrils,

unspoken mouthfuls

looming large
resounding
underneath
green
thunder's breath,

the current's
cursed occurrence
pulls down
overhanging branches
that had
recently
had
regal witness,

bearing fish:

fidgeting
through mist.

Splash!

Brown carp leaps

in eddy's
rippling spot
encircled
and outspreading
into bliss
of
lapping blast,

a
swell spill
of
innocent resistance,

reticent
in light
of
recent
light's reflection
crystalline
in water's
broadest
sparkling bands
broadcast passed
corners twisted,
brought downcast
after
gravity's
fantastic tug
downstream
had
toughed
it out

so
roughly
constant,

constantly unshaven,

forecast viciously

as maps
declare
the simple
methods
protocols
and
crude behaviors
of the
gradually ranging
reasons for
relationships
of elevations
unencumbered
by resistance

for an instant

at an instant

lest one
fear another's
pouncing truth
foretold;

then
bought,
then sold
by ounces

bouncing underneath
junked drainpipe
disappearing into

the most
(un)likely
brown(ish)
roiling of
surprising tremors'
smooth disturbances,

tender eyes
surprised
by mystery
of
temporary misperceptions,
on the watery
and the deep.

Every river has a way of talking.

Ask me
if
I'm listening
to the
slip
of
gravel
underneath
my feet,

confounding
waterfalls of
smooth stones
cracked
by winter's

icy wedge.

This
river's
birth's
unearthed as
sudden breath
of sighing
earth we
hear as
gurgling in
evidence of
ankle-stain.

The rhythms'
wave
of
wavering breeze
almost hovers
near banks;

each twisting
comfort
a caress,

each
back-handed
eddy

edifying
dampened skin

of land,

engraving
toneless tomes
in timeless voices

as if the cattails had cried me a river.

Starshine glow
of sunset's undertow
is not so much a danger

as a rhythmic stillness

when croak

of
night heron
echoes
creaking cheep
of
tree frog

and even
crickets
come to
incandescent plainchant

surrendering

cadential

into
savage navigations

and

distilled

in
average acidity

of our
morose

and

basic adages…

…he just keep rolling…

…he just keep rolling along…

Great Blue Heron.

Still.

Great Blue Heron.

Undistracted.

Still.

So which

     came first?

        The river

          or

            the song

around it?

Allegro Marcato

syntactic's

                          fluid quick

guerrilla verbing

                          wordspews rivers

widened off forgotten tongues

              and strident as the melt of days

              in youth's exotic wordchoice.

              ungodly hand's informal touch

                (in elderly translations)

                  reverent

irreverent—**NEWSWISE**—(stop)lines

              shouting words on *WORDS*

so (**stop(!)**)

              the absence of all breath

                (once thought as **DEATH**)

was all along the rumbling up

the ceaseless lavas of invention

cooling soon aneutral'd

(but much darker than the pitchwhite face

of untyped page's **BLANK,**

entombing

legend

of obsession).

everything's (of course!) unfinished,
but off course
stanzas (windows seen)
still reveal the iron screen
(a dry erase) condemning flying
words
to death starvation pressed like roses
trapped in books

at vague, unhappy avg.

you **KNOW** it's **TRUE(!)**
--**AND**--truth's a tuneful sideshow
callioping through the raw nerve fair.

love's detuned

by dint of chimney's

uneventful vent of smoke

(misfiring **FOG**)

esteemed but…(wrong?)

not for long!

riding on the air's awright
in place of creature comforts
and coming to
(as vague) as acid joys:

a smoothish imagery of blustered brash
blasts humidly
as motivation moderates
progressive matter's mutterings

in degrees

as hyphen's hoeish hopes
are madly dashed
and awled:

is all the rage encaged
in warps of skittish wordlings
shouting (**BACK!**)?
&

                              if riding unawares
                                    at night
                                replaces odd

                           (remember?)

                           features feebled on the face
                             of days we'd brandished,

scattered wonderings are seized
'til hope is sadly matched
by pound (**IV**)lb (**UN**
sound!) (re)birth
                                      'til yer riding
                             and you stare passed faces (odd?)
whenever tender meat
                             of fabled 'addled' weight of days'
                                outlandish brand of
                                    wanderings
                                    we sneeze into
                             a badly-worded mispronouncement
                                (unannounced trickstery)
                             'RELEVANT': recent renovations-
                             deconceals rezounding **SOUND.**

                                (sic) **transit!**

hence(forth) we must not worry
where the wordish slide may fall
for the novelty of vowel's

modifying constance
heaves in waves of gaping life
that pulls (**SPLAT**) like a
paintball knot of crows
or even theorhetoric's misguided arrows.

        in sequenced songlight
        sonneteers confuse
        the nounish nonforgotten,
        rottened, nourishmental state
        of adverse adjective's recalibrations.
        adverbs adding verbs return
        in swarms of sonic syllabrations
        spinning fullward leaps larruping up
        for sake of falling down,
        and after downcast dawn of sound
            bounds passed,
        comes flashing flush and fateful…

           heaving bashful **HATE**
          areddening ruddied cheeks
       (whence whistling) awhittled
            into song and dance-
         we tranced poetic transitives
      ((delicious(!) and licentious)ly)
     and thence were held (accountably)
        for unaccounted unpaid syntax.

Queer ache gyrate alphabet quiver.

Liquid ilk poison flange cosmic fizz!

Mystery persist!

Stiff glyph flotsam dawn laughter!

All myth satisfy nectar,
loft quill miser.

Agony kiss aroma bandit:
awful terror affair.

Bliss orchid;
rhythmic churn censor:
echo scam gala.

Guilty wobble?

Angry plastic weasel!
Secret wishbone puddle.

Ankle zither:
Speech lever nasty;
congregate diction racket.

Bottle destination acreage
into worldly velocity tower.

                              Next,

placid revelation stark uprising--
corridor vulture--
equalize breeding gaff.

Snowflake parade flesh device…

…destroy brief pose allergy,
aardvark abomination pairing.

Disease cushion poor night,
never strand amateur hint gambler.

Amusement:
death farm liberation.

Ape moon lung cascade.

Area murder coronation immunity.

Adequate baby switch poodle cloth.
Evil candy boot carcass?

Trust blockbuster bubblegum sunday,
helmet monkey!

Clown bargain depth pill!

Dynamite cubscout muffin,
literate mushroom pizzazz object.

Primal robot someone,
sharp seesaw will finger trim fruit,
wake high bug nonsense.
Touch pillow answer,
used picnic breath.

Wet backward body paste:
wide banana is daily wood blame!

Trouble outgrow glad butcher,
tease sincere mouth nervous.

Bypass shiny need.

Stop blossom soup.

Chew golden chipmunk chimney.

(Fear fathom thirst.)

Mix fast crayon,
promise thimble proud growl hook.

Lamb gallop,
lantern saucer.
Lick mirror plow.

Scrub perfect latent oven riddle.

Ring pretend recess.

Ripe scissors fail swim.

Hollow magic rubber we,

ugly tongue camera
whisper empty circus.

Melt wonder, cowboy.

Curb fierce mitten.

Old jungle blood scandal
squeeze thunder.

Slather kiosk ajar.

Absorb
still oil.

Drown coyote.

Lazy puzzle asks no home.

Birth--

how blaze bloom:

remember river

(electric flower)!

    Never would such

        worldly construct

           (whirling whiz

              of specious

(non(specific)))

will of wordish dervishes

                              seem omnistrictured

                    in our sweetly structured revelries.

an errant **REMNANT** word: incongruous--

          a congregation of weird syllabic lapfuls,
          archrival, long forgotten
                              (subtly said!) exasperations,
relaxed conflagrations (sudden recompense
                              for pensive, fearish flurries);

                                        could the
          strictly subatomic imparticulars
                                        matriculate
                              to paragraphs

                    (now paralyzed, unrealized)

               congealed?
footstep's trek's been beat
into travail of trails

                              as stone
                              to sand
                              to dust
                              to ash,

setting mouldered into winterish mush.

reactionary spit of reflex
vexes steel-toed boot embodied
by a kick at tricklish stones'
semi-sheltered morbid toes,
sending showers of chaotic gravel
tumbling to ellipses,
several semicolons and a set of dots
for dotish eyes--
pupil's outlined leaning lurch
smirks urgently and turgid...

be it comma's exclamation
animate and mammal-warm,
disconsonant;
who'll question con(pro)fusion
of these fissile tones we charm
into an incidental phrase or (worse)
replacement of an accidental grace
with saying(sing)s of

"Where & When...?"

and

'Which Were We?'

noun and verb technique
emits a quivering semi-quaver

of some semi-clever speak soon seen
ensconced (enshrined)
consigned to blithe denial
(**SMILE!**)

styled with a twist of curl,
a heedless heading:
herded (un)heard verses
(**WORD**((such)**CURSE**))
of nondiscursive pursing lips
pursuing flippant flip of tongue
until we've begun describing unenlisted
even (**more**) unspeakable images
we (just as well) could point to.

Presto

As April chill descends around my knuckles
and light lingers at the point of evening
the wind that seeps through window's screens
swirls room's smoke
until the Winter air escapes.

I stare at paper

wrinkled or unwrinkled,

pull cigarette from pack and light,

rerefreshen cup of coffee,

change again
the mood of tape

and stare at wrinkled paper.

In a world of typewriter monkeys
one of us was bound to stumble onto this,
resulting
in a stub-toed 'nnghh'
and so we aped it
and we eked it out
into a warning;

a footnote to the day.

Some mid-stoned aging tribe
could have discovered
that a snarl

followed by a grunt
(or grunts) could help
coordinate a shift or push
of rock or fallen tree.

Maybe

some wavers
in an ancient gesture language
learned
through trial and repetition
that a certain mumbling hum
becalmed a startled child.

It seems more likely
that the peacock dazzle
of our throaty affirmation
fortified a strutting springtime rut.

Years of parroting parade into parody
in purity of parts we've played:

the countless roles we've roosted in,

the many rules we rode o'er

gone apeshit batty
and hysterical reclusive.

I wouldn't just be thinking wishful;
lending undue character
to some dumber beasts than we

if the Doolittle in me
perceived a pattern
waiting weighted
in these patchworks of societies:

How do white cells spot disease?

Flowers' singing nectar's heard by hummingbirds
and bees.

Why do Grizzlies claw at trees?

Gombe's chimps may shriek and mutter constantly,
but their communicatin's telling more
by outstretched hand
and sincerity of eyes.

Remember, now,
we've even put collective ear to ocean,
hearing whalesong 'til we realize
near every critter
drums up a growl or purr
or flare of teeth
when putting instinct's mind to it.

Our personal complexities
just pooled it into lexicographies.

These theories of conspiracies:
let's leave them be.

It's like this, see:

Once
water would suffice.

Then,
we rediscovered ocean
and found we needed
salt and sweet.

Next we knew,
we fell
reigned in by rain

and then one day:

it snowed;

we just spun it out from there

and there it goed...

until our greatest prophets
started hearing voices
in stormclouds and brushfires,
warning and informing us
that earth is Shiva's regal yo-yo.

Symbols like metaphors
and expand into associations

until Everything's involved

and impish self

enthralls us into
bliss of myth.

We ought to now confess
the blessed streamlined patchwork acreage
we grew into a modern usage
irrelevated extra breaths,
sucked out listless letterings...
but overlonged our prologue
with prescient prefixes
that fused with passing swathes of suffixry
until the painful calibrations
of our simple congregations
congealed into a conflagration
of vague
and overnonspecifically engaging
paragraphs and tendencies:
a cotton candy web of words stuck
on you like friendly conversation.

We spin sugary words into the void
and whistle exhaled air
through strange-shaped mouths
striking acrobatic fun.

Dazzlingly new expressions
seep into a rippling tide of songpaint.

Each new poem piles onto each
the last sedimentally inscribed
and sentimental as a sigh.

It's best we let the tangles lie
in graveyards
of forgotten dictionaries
where spiteful words retire
growing (tired-
anthropomorphed until)
endlessly enraptured;
disingenuous is
freedom's swell and adjectival ebb.

Disembodied vocalese gusts through window's screens

like choking radiator nightmare's
quaking sad impatience;

like industrial smoke and engine coolant's
lonely mongering among the vagaries of art
and decaffeinate truth scratched symphonic,

crafted into textures rough and loud
backgrounded by a carnival of sound.

Alive! and winsome,
itching icons on picture postcards
and in letters full of letters
shifting through shadows
in live black and white
hiding grey fog rapture
with a weary eye half mad
and mostly
satisfied until disgusted,
entrusted,

crusted and abused
by random tonguing's lashing,
and the lashes 'round the eye of storm
swarm delighted and beknighted
'round discussions tabled.

Disenfabled peaks in dreams
absolve themselves in words
imaginarily spelled and schemed.

Anthologized poetic steam's been vented
'til prevented.

Recirculating subjects through revisions
'til we've circumvented Vision's sum,
some recede to grey of city's smoke.

Pages torn and taped,
cut from early evening's stroll,
in stages plumped,
then withered.

Those embryonic messages
massaged the heartless ego
of a communicable species,
tho' it only served as chump change;
wicked tingling a-tinkling
in the pocket of a pair of pants or
sporting coat discarded by some other voice

and spit into an anxious ear:

as dreams comply
a moment is enough
to shake the thunder from the sky!

Frantic travelers trade language as currency
in currents and in waves.

Word games spin confounding eddies;
roil unfound sounds into decidedly less random mists
until our fishnet's filled
with new ways for describing things.

Somewhere...

the river that began in upper cold spring snow
or from emptiness of lake
is caused into a damned reservoir
or locked-up water's highway.

Reminiscences' incessant reminiscence
squawks fondly of rain
the day a rush of conversations overspilled,
then busted through completely.

This ceaseless, cluttered chattering
is sonic ammunition for the pale
distorted background growl
that adds up to our conception.
We would compromise integrity of structure
if we just ignored the talking talkers
factoring it out;
enabling and stabling the frame

we stretch our color-sodden quilt upon.

And at last:
this white noise traffic
is the liquid pulse
of fetus's enwombed entombment.

Frankly,

voices fill the silence in.

Such encouragement we got
from our collection of courageous words
surviving in a turbulence
of circumspect perspectives;

a buoyancy of languid
lollygagging rolls
across a wistful
twist of tongue.

These words won't work
unless one works at them.

Better yet,
these words
won't work
if everyone
must work
so hard
at them.

Oftentimes these words won't work.

They will not stick to you like burrs
unless they's sticky like molasses.

Our mad accomplishment
is more
than just
a cluttered list
dealph'betized
and bloated.

Scheming opposites in corners
as two urchins might,
the push and pull of dull expressions,
the tug of disparate, bashful,
needless leanings
stretches syllables to pieces
puzzlingly fatigued.

Curiosity
urged specificity
then sounded it out
in shades.

We not going crazy.

We come crazy.

To sing one's name's an ode to springing
as it's bringing you into the moment
when another's movement 'round you
dazzles your bedraggled mood until,

intending to be clever
and unsteady as enduring dreams,
you lapse into a senseless breathing pattern
that, through repetition, causes
an exhaustion of perception's gleanings.

And all of this
as passersby
gasp by.

Exhausting as it is,
each corner spun
can take you
in and out of sunlight
or even stun you
with a sudden
gust of wind.

Deepened,
this well of vocabularic shadings
broadens into macrocosmic grin.

Feverish and excited into song and dance,
we twostep dizzily.
Meanwhile,
muttering almost imperceptibly;

last-calling dreams

and falling fast
into a politiktok
dance of ink-dry pen's

excited, pensive reminiscences unrealized
like DNA's unblemished melting
upside down.

Imagine:
unimaginable
imagination's
image's
impressive
magic.

Such maddening majesty twirls
recklessly into a dervish swirl of
variations so depraved and so sincere
it's floating on a list of derivations,
so severe

it's tenderizing old wound's words.
it's elusive as a shell game
and exotic fresh and charming.
it's secret as the secrets of a tidal pool.
it's inscrutable as cat purrs.
it's named with pale consistency
and sometimes called as myth
but is generally accepted legend.
it's never as emotional as implied.
it's set and pasted into order,
martyred into visionary shapes and depths.

and

it's deceptive as the teller in his tone,
as tender as his sense of nuance
will allow.

Until neurotic cigarettes alight, enlightened by a perfect
        match;
Until we recapture captivated self from television
        keenly tuned to last night's drama and watched
        by the sad sofa;
Until gold diggers and diamond miners pick their
        noses in public;
Until this hollow, floating mist of misperceptive
        messages darting forth and back in blackface
        drifts unmissed (perhaps misled) to dreamcharts
        of edible poetry wailing unwritten in a kinder-
        garten in Iowa;
Until that uncertain perfect sense of bestiality thickens
        air, humidifying sickly fogs with sweetened sec-
        rets of forbidden passion;
Until we organize discolored photographs of ancient
        anarchists, our heroes merely choking, poison
        pill placeboes swallowed whole;
Until libraries fill with emptied books devoured and
        envisaged as the vintage texts;
Until surprised antagonists beseech us be they unbathed
        unbelieved or even unromantic;
Until we hyperbolic hams cry laughishly, unwinding
        slavish luster as a wounded bounty on our pouting
        puppeteers;
Until we're somewhat psychotic and we're very bored;
Until limp wicked mystics flee the neon oasis, selling
        blind pencils in broken alleyways, chainsmoking

in the thick air of basements glued to numbers,
shades of archaic lettering gone to dust and toenail
clippings;
Until we grow massive in the caverns of subway sun-
light echoing through holes and pits like Casey
Jones gone around the bend;
Until we are glorious in the windows and at the glass-
works, reminded of the mindlessness of bloody
feet on long sand beaches;
Until we smell of free abandoned furniture rain-soaked
bright and shaking under thunders of eclectic
pleasure;
Until we Picasso through deserts and dampen soils dark as
shapes of mountains;
Until we learn to dance in churches blue as the night and
sidewalk swiftly through labyrinths of prismsong;
Until we contemplate a pilgrimage to Graceland;

We are desperate skeptics spitting death.

We are jazz hawkers in the carnival of shame.

But we are hyperactive hypochondriacs in drunken
hospitals goosing nurses and engraving sonnets
on bedpans and inscribing obscene odes in tapi-
oca pudding demanding that we

free everyone:

Because everyone is accidentally free already
Because even the void and demented night should cease
come morning

Because the stars still shine even in the city where mists
        break 'til low-slung planets bust through
Because in the blue of morning these stars dim and sigh
        like the final humdrum bananas browned on the
        shelf now sweet enough to eat near free
Because bare-naked angels taunt me silently somber in
        the sorrowful trees
Because the clouds smoke us a thousand vivid sculptures
        of youth torment
Because water just falls from the sky every time it rains
Because the color of thunder makes the sky spill out all
        her blue
Because the feckless autumn leaves leave me incurably
        worried in the lands condemned incurably calm
        as the naked native sun
Because sudden flutes mimic the moon's mystery foot-
        steps on nightlit sidewalks disinterested cries
        horning in on brief smitten time
Because of the basic needful wander of bright dust on
        forbidden paths near railroad tracks that never
        bend but drift smaller and smaller pointed to
        the west where the land cries like music
Because unleavened love lies flat as the pancake sun a
        harsh awakening of unlidded eyes in the brusk
        morning dew
Because the curious design of shadows in tree-filled
        parks sits forever waiting proof for words of
        amity a catchall waistband elastic latched to
        bystanders like catcalls
Because peppery lips smell salty frontal matter like a
        nosebleed stopt and clogged to the vein
Because arbitrary symbols of other things tangle in

the underbrush of sidewalk breakthroughs
like weeds and grasses left nothing between
here and now
Because fishhooks and more functional labels paste on
like pigeon's leavings on statues, stoics and
others as slothful
Because given the more chiseled features of desultory
time even palmistry grows lunatic in decadent
decades
Because rustic fascinations shiver logic in us like ran-
dom kernels or sudden peevish voices
Because some tangent to pelvic ruminations like the
whish of war dance, territorial smocks stiff
with blood like paint or dust squelched like
rain dripped from umbrella to stovetop
Because the evenhanded tone of the sky vexes even
the wasted elders bereft in the moth-eaten
expression of time
Because in odors are heard the blind messages of tired
cities cracked under soot and under foot found
crushed are the vivid spiders of violent and
religious devotions

Because as she used to say

There's just one way
to sing a senseless song
around the cloud's
steady busker
'crost the mildewed midnight
full-mooned sky.

Because one time said is crazy

and two times said is habit,

three times said

will

set you

get you

freedom.

Jim D. Deuchars is an American poet from Waukesha, WI. His work has appeared in a variety of print and online journals. He has released over a dozen books of poetry, including *Mockingbirds Contemplating Semicolons* (Kung Fu Treachery Press, 2020). Dismissive of the tribalism that divides the various schools and cliques of contemporary poetry, Deuchars embraces a wide variety of style, technique, and wordplay to craft poems that resonate equally in academic and outsider circles. Mixed with a generous portion of humor, this results in work that has been described as, "a special brand of doggerel, nonsense & foofaraw."

This project was made possible, in part, by generous support from the Osage Arts Community.

Osage Arts Community provides temporary time, space and support for the creation of new artistic works in a retreat format, serving creative people of all kinds — visual artists, composers, poets, fiction and nonfiction writers. Located on a 152-acre farm in an isolated rural mountainside setting in Central Missouri and bordered by ¾ of a mile of the Gasconade River, OAC provides residencies to those working alone, as well as welcoming collaborative teams, offering living space and workspace in a country environment to emerging and mid-career artists. For more information, visit us at www.osageac.org

Osage Arts Community